SOCCER SHORT STORIES FOR KIDS

Charlotte Gibbs

TABLE OF CONTENTS

INTRODUCTION

Imagine yourself standing in the middle of a soccer field; it's a bright, sunny day. Can you hear the roar of the crowd? Are you excited or calm as you mentally prepare for the match to start? Your heart beats hard as you wait for the excitement of the game to begin. Today will be your day to shine. You can feel it!

You focus on the ball in the middle of the field, tune out the noise, and get ready to help push your team to victory. Join me on the pitch—or rather, in this book—on this journey into the tales of this dazzling cast of characters, players who overcame adversity and challenging upbringings, and inspired fans worldwide with their extraordinary skills. Will you join me in learning about their goals and dreams, and what motivated them to focus on making them all come true?

Kids in playgrounds, fields, and streets from all corners of the globe practiced their game, launching headers and kicking balls at walls or through their opponents' legs. They daydreamed about winning the big game and waved their jerseys in the air as they slid across the grass to celebrate the game-winning goal.

The beautiful game, as it is sometimes called, has been around for at least 3000 years. The Aztecs had a version of soccer known as Tchatali—the game was sometimes used in rituals to honor the sun and featured a bouncing ball made of rubber (most early cultures didn't use rubber at the time). In China, around 300 BC, players played a version of the game inside a square and used a ball made of stitched leather and stuffed with fur or feathers. While Aboriginals in Australia played a style of the game called Marn Gook—the goal of the game was to keep the ball airborne!

I've got a question for you. Why is the game called soccer in some places and football in others?

Around 1863, an English association helped make the word "soccer" go viral as it started to be used as a nickname for a local organization. As the word gained popularity, it became the standard way to help people from mistaking the game for other forms of football like rugby and American football.

We'll read about players like Kylian Mbappé, the lightning-fast forward from France. Or, Lionel Messi, the confident legend from Argentina. Or, how about you "step over" to Cristiano Ronaldo's fast feet? Wait, you're into legends like Megan Rapinoe or Christine Sinclair, aren't you?

I'm sure you are!

If magic and superstition are more your thing, tales of charms, predictions, and truces will appear too! Tales of high scores and low moments hide in these pages, and you'll be awed, humbled, or charmed by the groundbreaking achievements.

What dreams pushed these superstars to succeed? What motivated these players to grow up and hold championship after championship over their heads?

Reading these stories will inspire and help you use your hearts, minds, and voices to inspire positive change.

CHAPTER 1

HEY NOW, WHAT'S THAT VUVU-SOUND?

The song of the vuvuzela is going on. And on. And on. Everyone had an opinion. "Hey, I really like this sound!" some would say, while others were a bit confused: "Is there something broken?" They checked their TVs and looked around at each other, stumped. "Oh, wow! Oh, no! What are we going to do?" many wondered.

Let's take a step back for just a moment.

So, historically, you would listen to the beat of the drums and the (shall we call it buzzing?) of the vuvuzela as part of healing rituals during special services held by African church leaders before it became popular with many African soccer teams and their fans in the 1980s.

So, here we are in 2010, and World Cup fever has taken over South Africa. Can you imagine how excited they were to introduce the vuvuzela to the world? The vuvuzela is something so true to their culture and history. It is bold, loud, and impossible to ignore. It would be the most exciting moment for them as they shared something they treasured so much with all soccer fans worldwide.

What do you think happened next? Fans worldwide started tuning in and were surprised to hear a unique sound blaring from their televisions. Buzz, buzz, buzz! Is it an attack of killer bees? Many wondered and hoped they wouldn't have to listen to that sound for the entire tournament.

Spoiler alert: oh boy, did they ever!

Even the players had a few less-than-kind words to describe their experiences on the pitch—they criticized the use of vuvuzelas during the matches because it made it harder for the players to communicate. Some players were unhappy that the vuvuzelas made their jobs more difficult, and teams blamed their losses on the overwhelming sound. A few players, though, were open-minded and admitted that it was hard to deal with, but it was important for players also to respect the way the culture chose to celebrate.

After its grand "opening," many fans were "intrigued" by its unique sound. To no one's surprise, the poor vuvuzela wasn't invited to the 2014 World Cup (just in case you missed the sound or thought the sound was edited out!) and has been banned at dozens of sports events and stadiums since.

Here's to hoping a quieter version will make a comeback! It made that World Cup very memorable!

Being unique, humble, and grounded is required. Sometimes, it's hard to prove yourself. It's easy to forget that you didn't achieve your goals by luck alone. Remember, you made it because you were focused and worked hard. While so many people love the vuvuzela, many fight against it. This is an excellent example of everyday life. Sometimes, when we are so eager to embrace something, we are surprised when people fight back.

How can you be a shining example? By having a positive attitude, being passionate, and being dedicated. Remember that as you figure out your dreams, like the vuvuzela, others may not realize what makes you unique and why you celebrate your history and accomplishments the way you do. Know that there are endless possibilities and paths you can choose. Always motivate yourself to be the best version of yourself you can be, and don't let your age or background stop you from pursuing your passions and putting your best foot forward! Start each day with the confidence of the player who gets the first kick-off of the game. By staying humble, focused, and hardworking, you will get to score in life!

Words to live by, right?

CHAPTER 2

IS IT IN? OR IS IT OUT? GHOST GOAL

In the early 90s, two German teams, FC Bayern Munich and FC Nurnberg, faced each other. Each team had its eyes on glory, determined to win. However, glory wasn't meant to be that day; it was not in the cards. Twenty-five minutes into the game, a Bayern player tried tapping the ball into the net, and it looked like it just squeaked in.

It's a goal! Or is it? Did that ball really go in? The referees discussed it briefly before deciding the goal was good. That "good" goal was not good, and a new word, "Phantomtor," was born to describe this odd occurrence. Now, it had to be something bizarre for people to create a new word because of it, wouldn't you say? Imagine the confusion and irritation of the players as they tried to decide whether it was a goal.

So, what happened? As they say in showbusiness, the show must go on, and in the sports world, it is the same. While the players were frustrated and confused, the game simply continued. Well, the game ended, and the debate began. If the "Phantomtor" hadn't counted, the match would've been a draw instead of a win for Bayern. As this was a critical game, it needed a clear winner.

After a review by the German Football Association, they ordered a rematch. Can you imagine being one of the players who played in the original game? Would you be angry or relieved when you heard you had to play again? The players expressed both emotions. Some were annoyed because they felt their team deserved the victory, but other players were thankful for the chance to try again.

Bayern had to face Nurnberg again, but thankfully for them, Bayern Munich won the game easily by a score of 5-0. It took another 20 years for the term 'ghost goal' to become famous in pop culture when Chelsea's manager, Jose Mourinho, used it after Liverpool's win against Chelsea during a league championship game. If you think that a ghost isn't usually associated with soccer, you are 100% right. But this makes us wonder: What is a ghost goal?

Unlike its spooky name, a ghost goal has nothing to do with ghouls, goblins, witches, or spirits. Although, like their spooky counterparts, these ghost goals are always haunted and cause a fright because the ball tends to develop a mind of its own (no matter how well placed the strike), leaving players and fans alike shocked and scratching their heads. These players might feel that a ghost is sneakily kicking the ball.

Seriously, though. What is a ghost goal?

A "controversial" element of the game that can often sway the match's outcome is a ghost goal, which is a goal given when the ball doesn't cross the line or when a goal that does cross is taken back.

Despite the occasional frustration caused by these bloopers, they do make for good memes! Whether it's the non-goal, the fans in the stands, the players' witty or snarky remarks, or the coaches' frustration on the sidelines. Sport is like everything in life. We need to take the good with the bad. That is why even the blunders matter. Players can learn from them, and fans might enjoy a giggle, too.

Depending on who you're cheering for, another highlight (or lowlight) happened during the 2010 World Cup. It was a big matchup, a knockout elimination match! England vs. Germany, nearing the 39th minute and roughly 50 seconds after Matthew Upson scored England's first goal of the match. Frank Lampard has the ball, dribbles it closer and closer, and he boots it! Oh, it looks so good; that ball is in! Well, not so fast, sports fans, even though it clearly hits the underside of the crossbar, and just as it's about to cross the line into the net, an odd backspin sends the ball onto the pitch! The (non) goal, sometimes called "Wembley goal reloaded," didn't count—if it did, England would've tied the game at 2-2. Unfortunately for English fans, Germany went on to win 4-1.

To prevent this kind of drama and heartbreak, leagues far and wide thought long and hard about ways to combat and find a way to avoid ghost goals, eventually pushing for rules that allow for goal-line technology such as VAR (video assistant referee).

Challenge yourself to explore what success and failure mean to you. Does it have a lot or a bit of value? It can spark happiness and heartbreak, and it may take time to figure out how to crush your disappointments. It takes courage and builds character when you remain hopeful and resilient. As you navigate unpredictability, stay inspired and remember that life, like a match, has wins and losses. What matters is that slips and setbacks can be the magic (drive) you need to succeed. Remember, winners are not people who have never been disappointed or struggled. Instead, they are people who refuse to give up no matter how hard things are. So, even when things are hard, tell yourself you are a winner, too, and push through! You can do it!

CHAPTER 3

I SING, YOU SING, WE SING

We all have dreams that we hope will come true. In fact, if you had to close your eyes and think about your biggest dream, there is no doubt that you could bring it to mind easily and that just thinking of this dream would put a smile on your face. In February 2024, a longtime fan dreamed a dream, and her wish was granted. Fans in the crowd held their red and white scarves in the air as their voices rang loud and true. Angels? No, only people taking a moment to kindly grant a fellow sports enthusiast her dearest wish, a way to remember for a beat when she once sat in the crowd and cheered on her team! For a moment in time, back inside a stadium where she spent decades enjoying the gift of song—a beautiful moment, not a dry eye to be found. Imagine being in the crowd, amongst a haunting yet pretty uproar, a heartfelt chant, a musical wave called the Mull of Kintyre.

Almost 20 years ago, a lifelong Nottingham Forest supporter gave up her season's tickets because she was losing her ability to see. Now, the idea of being unable to see is a scary thought for anyone. Sight is such an essential part of our daily lives that it is nearly impossible to imagine our lives without it.

Sadly, this fan had to accept the idea of being unable to see. She loved listening to the tune. Sure, she could listen as much as she wanted to at home, but sometimes, she didn't want to listen to the announcers' stories; do you blame her? They were talking over the Mull of Kintyre, which just wouldn't do. So, she begged her daughter to drive up to the stadium and park as close as possible so she could hear the rallying cry live instead of on television.

The fan, now blind, was so happy to be so close, but her family had other ideas. One more chance to be inside the stadium, they planned and planned. Just one more chance to hear the Mull of Kintyre, her team's rally song, in person. As luck would have it, her favorite team, Forest, was more than delighted to oblige! This shows the beauty of sportsmanship. Sport brings us all together and makes us stronger as a unit. It's not about doing something for yourself but rather about helping everyone.

Mull of Kintyre has been the team's anthem since the late 1970s. It is also a song by a famous band called Paul McCartney and Wings. While Forest's and Wings' versions of the Mull of Kintyre may differ, both are about love. For the band, it was about enjoying, living in, and loving the remote peninsula in Scotland—the anthem is more about loving and standing by your team during its ups and downs.

Now, let's meet its American cousin, a cheer called I Believe.

Say it with me. It's a pretty easy chant to follow. We'll start with, I. And then we'll keep adding words until we're saying the whole sentence; I believe we will win!

Are you ready? Great! Here we go!

I
I Believe
I Believe We
I Believe We Will
I Believe We Will Win!

Wasn't that fun? It's not what you expected, I'd bet. Can you picture yourself in a stadium screaming it with thousands of other fans? Chants like this one bring people together and keep the excitement of sport alive!

Commercials featuring the chant were made in 2014 to cheer on the US Men's National Soccer team, who adopted the chant. The women's national team adopted the chant, too; during a victory parade, the team led the crowd in cheering: I believe we just won! The chant even became a popular hype-motivational song. The power of music is such a gift to us. If you ever have to run a race and feel tired, play your favorite music. You might be surprised by the burst of energy you get from listening to the music. Music makes us happy and enthusiastic. When it comes to sports, music also binds us in wonderful ways.

Oh, the power of a song (or a chant), the feeling of belonging, is vital to loving a sports team. Would you be moved to tears? (Our dear Forest fan was, in case you were wondering. Her daughter was delighted to see her mom so happy!)

What do you notice about your favorite soccer team (or player)? You may notice (or feel) a sense of belonging; unity connects sports fans regardless of their histories, experiences, or backgrounds. Inspiring! Anthems, rally cries, and chants are also a wonderful experience to share with thousands of other people, and in a small way, they give you hope, besides the hope that you can will your team to win. It's the hope that being a part of something will give you the courage to achieve anything you put your mind to, to push for goals greater than yourself, more than you believed possible.

CHAPTER 4

FROM ME TO YOU, FOR YOU TO ME

You take mine, and I'll take yours. Let's remember this moment forever!

No one knows for sure, but historically, it's documented that the first jersey swap occurred around 1931. France was overjoyed because they had beaten England for the first time and wanted something to remember the moment! It's pretty cool that the English players were kind enough to agree! Hopefully, the English team held on to the French jersey, too. Sure, it may not have meant as much, but the gesture is so kind that why not keep it to remember the moment? Sport isn't just about who is victorious. It is about helping each other be the best version of ourselves. The English team's willingness to swap jerseys shows that they understand that it is about more than who scored the most goals. It is about being supportive, humble, and helpful.

Did you know the jersey swap didn't make its "debut" in the World Cup until 1954? But that wasn't the most famous—that one was in 1970 when legends Pele and Bobby Moore swapped jerseys.

Picture an intense rivalry between two legendary teams, England and Brazil. Brazil pulled off a 1-0 win in a game that featured more of the bad side vs. the good side of the beautiful game—including flops, fierce hits, and hot tempers. Even with this rivalry, Pele and Moore put their differences aside to create a moment many fans still cherish.

Pele and Moore took off their shirts and hugged each other in a moment that showed their mutual admiration. This gesture showed the power and magic of sports when one puts differences aside to foster sportsmanship and respect.

While the above example shows how this exchange should go, sometimes a little confusion can make the best intentions go south. During the 2018 World Cup, Australian soccer player Jason Cummings wanted to exchange jerseys with a player on the French team. First, he set his sights on Kylian Mbappé, but it didn't work out. So he tried asking Olivier Giroud instead. Unfortunately, there was a bit of a mix-up, and Cummings didn't get the jersey. Maybe distraction, lack of active listening, or plain old tiredness after the game caused the issue.

Things may have gotten a little heated, and Cummings felt snubbed. However, it was a misunderstanding, and a few tweets later, they hashed it out. A few years passed before the players swapped jerseys in 2023. Cummings received a Giroud AC Milan jersey, and Giroud received a Cummings Central Coast Mariners jersey—a lovely way to get past the misunderstanding and become friends. This is an excellent example of how technology and sports can be helpful in our lives. If it wasn't for the ability to connect through Twitter, the misunderstanding of what happened on the field would not have been resolved, leaving a bad taste in the players' mouths.

Sure, the jersey is "only" a uniform, but it's also more than that. A jersey is a piece of clothing that makes a person become an idol, revered by many people. It is also a symbol of identity, passion, and shared loyalty, and swapping them becomes a way to tell and share stories and embrace and value everyone's journey. A team's jersey is also more than just a symbol for the individual players. It is a symbol of unity and teamwork.

The jersey swap is a simple act that teaches us that finding compassion and balance can be as simple as giving the shirt off your back to your opponent after a game. It is as simple as letting go of any grudges and celebrating a moment that, on the one hand, once mattered more than anything and, on the other, doesn't mean much after it's all said and done. The jersey is now a symbol that reminds you to embrace differences and focus on being open-minded.

The jersey confusion also teaches us that we should try to avoid making assumptions as much as possible. By going according to what we think could have happened and not checking the facts, we can make ourselves and those around us unhappy. Instead, by checking in and clearing the air, we are ready to make the most of every day and build friendships that last a lifetime.

In a small way, every jersey tells a story—memories of wins and losses, bonds that will never be broken, the value of hard work, and the power of teamwork.

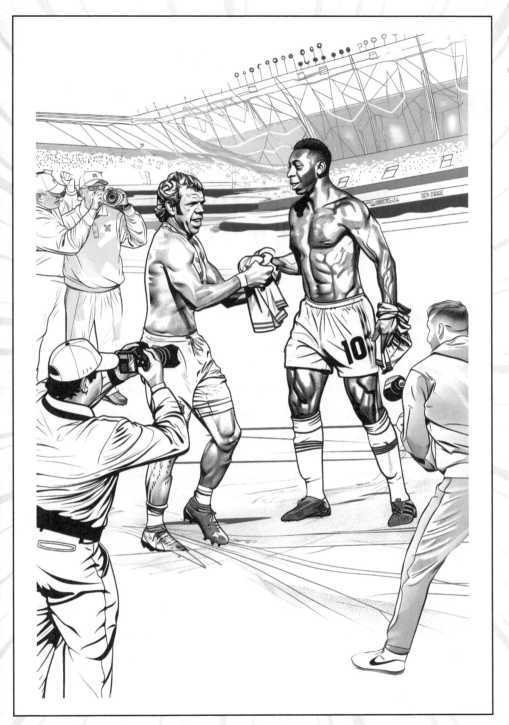

CHAPTER 5

UNMELLOW YELLOW AND A BLUE RED CARD

Times were tough, tension filled the air, tempers were hot, and long-standing rivalries were part of the game—being calm and collected wasn't in the cards. Let's say no one remembered or always had the time or patience to aim to be nice. Heads were scratched, and boy, something needed to change. But what? It had to be something bold, like how the Elastico move faked out defenders on the pitch.

What reprimand would do the trick? As the saying goes, the punishment (to teach the appropriate lesson) has to fit the crime (the infraction); it has to stand out and make the players realize they have gone too far. Decisions, decisions, decisions.

First, a little history.

During the 1966 World Cup, bad tempers dominated the quarter-final match between England and Argentina. Confusion, followed by frustration, fell over the pitch, and the referee, exasperated, sent off an Argentine player. The player was upset. He felt the referee was trying to help England win the game.

After the game, the referee spent a lot of time stumped. Remember, it is not just the players who care about the game. Referees are just as passionate and committed to the sport. That is why he just couldn't let it go. Two questions kept him up at night. What could he do to make the game better? What could he do to make things easier in the future? While sitting at a stoplight one day, a cautionary (think yellow) idea started to form—using yellow might be a bright way to give a warning, and if the behavior got worse, then red would mean the end, and the player would be out of the game.

Unsurprisingly, there were ups and downs, hills and valleys, misdirections, and clear offsides as the card system was being figured out. After a few years, the system debuted and was quite successful at first. However, like some of your favorite superheroes (or villains), too much power started corrupting a few too many referees, and they used that power to control games. To save the game, the card system was retired. As you already know from watching soccer games, the card system thankfully came out of retirement, those dastardly hiccups were defeated, and the system was reborn in better (fighting) shape.

Speaking of shape, imagine being in no shape to be a referee and, in an angry fit, giving yourself a card and ejecting yourself from the game. Yup, there have been a few cases of referees giving themselves a red card. In 2005, a referee lost his temper with the players after hearing one too many complaints; the final straw happened when the goalkeeper began protesting when his team was denied a free kick. Poor guy! He threw off his whistle and left the game. Once he left, the game had to end because no one was available to cover for the referee. It is important to remember that with positions of power comes great responsibility. Therefore, a referee should always aim to be fair.

Hopefully, you don't notice too much negativity in your world, but if you do, here's to hoping you already know that having an attitude or being negative isn't the way. It interferes with your growth, so don't hold on to anger. Let it go! By pointing out what you shouldn't be doing in these red card examples, here's to hoping their lessons will be lessons for you to know what not to do. Try your best to calm down before storming into or out of sticky situations, and always try to talk things through with a clear head, even if you have to talk about your feelings later. No team has a great time on the field every day. Some days are harder than others. The same applies to our daily lives. While today might be tough, tomorrow might be a great day. The key is to push forward and stay positive even when things are hard.

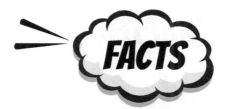

FACTS

1. Soccer is known as football in many countries, except in the United States and Canada. It's called soccer to distinguish it from American and Canadian football.

2. The first FIFA World Cup took place in Uruguay in 1930. The home country defeated Argentina in the final.

3. Pelé, the Brazilian legend, is the only player who won three FIFA World Cup titles. He was 17 when he won the first one, and by the time he was 30, he had already won the other two.

4. Almost 4 billion people worldwide play football, making it the most widely practiced sport.

5. The World Cup is the most-watched sports event in the world. It even surpasses the Olympics!

CHAPTER 6

GOALS GALORE

Soccer fans love the sport for its iconic moments, such as last-minute ties or shocking come-from-behind victories. Unlike basketball games, which often end with triple-digit scores, soccer games typically have lower-scoring affairs, with each team averaging one to three goals.

The style of play has undergone significant transformations, with shifts towards varying attacking styles, emphasizing flair, creativity, and a focus on scoring more goals.

What if I told you some soccer games have reached double digits, and one ended in triple digits? Yup! One game did just that! So, while not moments of beauty, nor moments when one is caught up in the tension of an evenly matched game, let's take a glimpse at events that may not quite reflect the sport's evolving nature. Instead of parking the bus and defending the keeper, let's go! Let's go(al) goal(ore) and read about several high-scoring goal extravaganzas!

Introducing the double-digit category: first, we have Arbroath FC. This Scottish team shot up the ranking recently and was nearly awarded a chance to become the first part-time team to play in the Scottish Premier League. Oh, so close! Arbroath indeed wanted (and needed) a clean sheet there! Better luck next time! Anyway, they are also known for their historic victory over Bon Accord in 1885, winning 36-0 during the first round of the Scottish Cup; this win remains the widest margin of victory in a competitive game to date.

Next is the highest known point differential in an international match, Vanuatu against Micronesia. Vanuatu won by nearly 50 points in the 2015 Pacific Games. What was the score? An unheard-of monstrous score of 46-0... oof! Micronesia didn't have a good time during this tournament; over three games, the team was outscored by 114 goals—with losses to Tahiti 36-0 and Fiji 38-0. Sadly, all those goals didn't help Vanuatu make it to the finals; they ended the tournament in third place because Fiji and Tahiti played to a nil-nil draw during a later qualifying game.

Oh yeah, here's the triple-digit game; you may notice that self-sabotage may make another appearance later on. Some may debate if this next game should be in the number one spot, but you can decide for yourself— it's a big number, a "numbers game, " and it's recognized in the Guinness Book of Records.

During a round-robin match in 2002, two teams faced off. One, AS Adema, had already advanced after a draw against the same team. Could this have inspired what was about to happen in that game? Their opponents, Stade Olympique de l'Emyrne, were out of the title race and, unhappy with poor calls from the referees in previous matches, decided to vent. In an odd twist, their protest was to constantly and repeatedly score own goals. The final score was 149-0, a record for the highest-scoring soccer game ever! After the game, the losing coaches and several players faced disciplinary actions.

How you choose to keep your emotions in check is a hard choice to make. In a perfect world, standing up for your beliefs should be easy, but you know it's challenging to find the right balance between using your power to make a difference and facing difficult consequences. Don't be discouraged; every step you take, big or small, makes a difference, even if it takes some time or others may not see things as you do.

Don't give up on your dreams; use these stories as a reminder that no matter what, always play fair. How we respond to our problems says a lot about who we are. It is important to stay true to your good values when you feel like you are losing the game of life. Remember that mistakes are a part of life. It is how we react and how much we learn from them that makes all the difference.

CHAPTER 7

FUN FACT CHECK—TO FINISH OR TO SHOOT

During World War II, when most men were either fighting the war or busy working, soccer adapted to the times, filling a gap that people in England needed to keep their hopes up. And why not use soccer? So, between 1939 and 1945, the Football League War Cup (FLWC) was born! The FLWC hoped to give English fans an alternative to the FA Cup (which was on hold during the war).

It worked! The first champion, West Ham, was crowned nine weeks after the tournament was created. Pretty fast, huh?

But in "not so fast" news, the game took forever to end, and after different ideas bounced around, in 1942, a new rule called "Play to a Finish" was born—extra time that didn't end; the game kept going and going. No one really took the time to think about "what if the game needed to end and took the time to create a rule that would end the game." The various teams quickly jumped on the bandwagon, and to everyone's surprise, the first few games went well. But not all things that start out well stay great, right? Can you guess what happened next?

As new ideas went, it was a great idea, until it wasn't; before long, games became messy and never-ending— imagine playing a game for over three hours, like Cardiff and Bristol City did, creating a new record. It didn't help that no one seemed to know what the rules were and kept making things up during games, just adding to the confusion. Imagine playing a game with players who are making up the rules as they go. It can be quite frustrating!

As that saying goes, all good things must come to an end, and the "Play to a Finish" rule was on its last legs. In March 1946, during a game featuring Stockport County and Doncaster Rovers. Stockport and Doncaster battled for a long time, with two games that ended in a 2-2 tie. The teams played past 'extra time' and kept on playing... and playing.

How long did they play for? About 203 minutes or almost three and a half hours—three minutes longer than the previous longest game record I just told you about! Why didn't the teams keep on playing? Unfortunately, it was too hard to see, and the smoke coming from the railway made it even harder for the already tired players to continue playing. So, to keep things fair, the officials (and players) decided to have a coin toss to decide who would host the rematch.

Doncaster won the toss, and the rematch was played four days later. Doncaster defeated Stockport 4-0. Local reporters, the fans, and the league were left shaking their heads in disappointment—what a horrible way to decide a game. To no one's surprise, the "Play to a Finish" rule ended a few months later. It is not really in the spirit of the game to fill people with disappointment or to give the element of luck so much power. Therefore, they knew something needed to be done.

Join me as we fast-forward to 1970. A group called the International Football Association Board (IFAB) decided that games shouldn't end in a tie (or draw). What did they think would spice the game up?

Penalty shoot-outs!

After being played in various leagues for about a decade, the penalty shoot-out was featured during the World Cup, Italia '90. Even though the players didn't like the shoot-out format at first, boy, did things get serious!

Enter Ireland, who wowed everyone when they stole the show against Romania during an exciting penalty shoot-out. This sparked a whole new way of thinking, forced teams to change their tactics, and ensured that mental and physical preparation became even more important (stories from the same tournament, like England's loss to Germany due to penalties, pushed teams to focus more than they had previously).

So, there you have it! From playing until the end, no matter how long it took, to the heartbreak (or joy) of penalties ending the game dramatically. Cool, huh?

Soccer teaches us a lot about finding our inner strength, honing our passions, and the magic we may find despite life's ups and downs. We should always remember to focus on being adaptable and brave to face challenges head-on. Also, we shouldn't forget that when things don't work out as planned, we shouldn't be defeated. Instead, we should look ahead and inside to find a way to make our spectacular comebacks, think outside the box (find opportunities in the bad times,) and push ourselves to make our dreams a reality! Being adaptable is very important because it helps us bounce back when things don't go our way. By being adaptable, we can embrace the changes that must be made and truly conquer every part of our lives.

CHAPTER 8

THE TRUCE GAME

Christmas is one of the most popular holidays around the world today. As a result, there are many amazing stories based on Christmas. Would you believe it if you heard that even a soccer story is told in the spirit of Christmas? Get ready to embrace the tale (or true story, possibly) of the Christmas Truce. Like every wonderful story, the Truce has been shared with and by generations of people, whether they heard it on the news or social media. From friends playing freeze tag to grownups in awe of the story, the story has traveled far and wide.

It focuses on a group of soldiers who found the courage to celebrate the season of giving. Prince William of England likes sharing the soldiers' tale to remind others about the power of sharing, fostering unity, and breaking down barriers to create a peaceful world that supports everyone's values. He also mentioned that keeping the Christmas Truce story alive is necessary because it's a message of hope for humanity in what can feel like dark and scary times.

You can imagine these poor men were unhappy spending Christmas Day in 1914 so far away from home. Maybe that's why it isn't hard to imagine what might have happened on those "sidelines." But we can imagine that the space dividing these two countries was the perfect place for a miracle to happen.

You have a lot of questions. Was it one big game with two teams battling it out? This is unlikely. Imagine how hard it would be to organize a game along a narrow 15- to 20-mile stretch. Instead, picture multiple games going on simultaneously: smaller groups of men using their coats or hats as goalposts; there probably weren't any referees, time limits, or scorekeeping, and for many, it was a well-deserved break.

Different groups of German and English soldiers played together, making up rules as they went along. Looking around at the different games, wondering where a ball came from. Or was that a rock? Nope, it's a few men using a tied-up sandbag as a ball. Have you ever heard the expression, "From necessity comes invention"? Well, that is exactly what happened at that time. Men used what they could find to bring their favorite game to life.

What if believing in the Truce had a deeper meaning? What could it be? Over 100 years after the Christmas Truce, a famous painting by John Singer Sargent underwent preservation; a previously "hidden" part of the painting suggested that soccer may have really been a pastime during the war. However, it's unknown if the Truce inspired the men playing soccer in the painting. If you want to see what the painting looks like, you can find it in an online gallery. Besides the painting, there are several statues and memorials around England commemorating the Christmas Truce, and in 2014, teams from the German and English armies participated in a friendly match.

So, I'll bet you're starting to wonder. Was there a game or not? Is there a clue you're missing? Or, like when a player discovers an opponent's "tell," maybe the Truce is a tale to make a sad time a bit happier, an imaginary event with just enough authentic details sprinkled in to spread Christmas magic.

The Christmas Truce is valuable because it shows the importance of finding ways to believe in and have faith in yourself. Its positive impact can help you learn what you can achieve when you open yourself up to wonder and magic. Remember, it's the act of believing that matters the most. What is the next step? Start by looking at yourself and focusing on things you can change instead of those you cannot. What examples do you set when life isn't going how you want it? How can you practice leading by example? Take a moment to reflect, look inside yourself, and focus on your inner dreams and wants. So stand tall, accept the (truce) truth, and don't give up!

The Christmas Truce is also an important story to share because it teaches us that connecting with each other makes a difference. Even if someone isn't on your team or a close friend, when we are united and work together, things are better for us all.

CHAPTER 9

SOCCER SUPERSTITIONS

People all over the world have superstitions. Whether it is being careful not to break a mirror or avoiding black cats and ladders, superstitions are fascinating. Do you have any superstitions? Would you be surprised to hear that soccer is filled with superstitions? Soccer superstition is a charming part of its culture; whether or not you believe in it is up to you. Superstitions range from quirky and lighthearted to customs based on meaningful rituals. Teams, players, and fans may add different spins to make the rituals more powerful because winning—no, sorry—unity is the building block that will bring glory to one's team.

Superstitions can be pre-match rituals that the players often repeat to ensure good luck triumphs over bad luck. Some players play music, others put their jerseys on head first, while others always put their left socks on before their right socks. Some prefer bringing lucky charms onto the field, like a coin or wearing jewelry; sometimes, the whole team is in on it. Some teams believe sitting in specific seats results in a victory. Don't be surprised if the seating arrangement remains unchanged until the luck wears off and the team experiences a loss.

A famous soccer superstition that many people believe in is the idea that bald players are good luck; think of Lucas Moura, who won a Summer Olympic silver medal, Fabinho, a Copa America runner-up, or Thierry Henry, who won two La Liga titles. This superstition has many origin stories and is believed to be known as "The Golden Egg," perhaps inspired by Aesop's fable… or maybe by a tale of a young man who shaved his head before a big game and scored the winning goal. Or, like the true story of France winning their first-ever World Cup in 1998 and the European championship two years later.

Many will have you believe that the key to France's success was the habit of kissing the goalkeeper, Fabien Barthez's bald head. Before games, his good friend, Laurent Blanc, would kiss the top of Fabien's head for good luck; eventually, the rest of the team did, too, and behold, good luck found Les Bleus. Unsurprisingly, many soccer players worldwide have adopted the bald look, inspired by ideas of luck, tradition, and a winning mindset.

Another unique superstition is that beloved animals can predict the outcome of games. Forget the ones who predict the weather, such as Wiarton Willie or Punxsutawney Phil. Soccer fans have celebrated animal oracles like Pulpo Paul (or Paul the Octopus in English), who correctly guessed the results of eight straight matches during the 2010 World Cup, and Achilles the Cat, who successfully predicted the winners of games during the 2018 World Cup. Lastly, hats off to the pet detective, Pickles. Pickles followed his nose and helped find the missing Jules Rimet trophy before the start of the 1966 World Cup.

Inspiration, like superstition, has many different forms. You can inspire through your efforts, your mindset, and what you treasure. Look around you; it isn't hard to find things to inspire and motivate you; it can be nature, being kind to or welcoming the kindness of strangers, or finding joy in the words of people you love. Your dreams, goals, and daily achievements can inspire you to push yourself whenever you face roadblocks. What else can you do? Try connecting to something outside yourself, then focus on gratitude and appreciating your accomplishments.

Why? It will create a positive attitude that will attract more positive energy. Gratitude reminds us that we can make a difference, big or small. It can help us find new ways of thinking, and you can use it to cultivate a growth mindset to help you navigate life's unexpected detours. So, maybe being superstitious is the writing on the wall that will force you to embrace and share your talents. Even if you are not a superstitious person, it is essential to be respectful of the beliefs of others. Open-minded people are more successful because they don't shoot others down just for being different. Instead, they embrace differences and grow with them.

CHAPTER 10

SAY HELLO TO THE REGGAE GIRLZ

One love, one heart, the Reggae Girlz from Jamaica stood together and engraved their names in hist-or-y. All right, here is a story I really have to share. It's a story of ladies who constantly had to face hopelessness and put their trust in a higher power (as well as themselves). These ladies joined together and created a kingdom of love.

Welcome to the story about a team whose chances kept thinning, who fought and didn't lose hope—their love of the pitch as beautiful as a group of four bobsledding men. Four men who clearly knew that they could overcome all obstacles in their way by focusing on that one love, by daring to get together to dream about bobsledding and breaking traditions.

Who are the Reggae Girlz? They're ladies whose spirits were as resilient as the country they represented. On the world stage, Jamaican heroism was on historic display—the women's national team stood determined to win! Picture the fans watching in awe while the "Reggae Girlz Rise Up," dribbling past any obstacles and odds stacked against them.

The Reggae Girlz had their team disbanded twice in two decades; isn't that heartbreaking? As devastating as this must have been, they did not give up. Instead, they were inspired more by this setback. Boy, did they work hard to bounce back. The team loved playing soccer so much that they were constantly fighting and fundraising to save their team from the brink. Thankfully, along with the support of local celebrities, the team managed to keep fighting, on and off the field. Despite and maybe even because of the external struggles, it took two tries for the national women's team to make it to the World Cup stage. Unfortunately, they didn't win any games the first time they qualified. The second time, though, the Reggae Girlz were more determined than ever— they pushed and pushed and pushed!

Throughout the group stage, the team didn't let any goals in. Would that be enough? Could the Reggae Girlz get past Brazil? As the clock ticked down, Jamaicans and soccer fans worldwide watched in anticipation. With less than a minute on the clock, nerves and worry filled the air—would Jamaica make it to the Round of 16? Thousands of eyes watched as that ball sailed through the air, a powerful shot from Brazil.

Forty-five seconds, then thirty seconds on the clock; it's like time slowed down as the ball raced through the air. Then, oh my God! Did you see that? The Jamaican goalkeeper made a game-saving stop. Jamaica came out victorious and advanced! They are indeed what we would call underdogs who got the bone!

Maintaining focus and mental strength when facing distractions is tough, but it's a valuable tool once mastered. Being adaptable and practicing your ability to concentrate and stay focused will help you block out outside distractions. It can help you bounce back from challenging situations, too. Now that you know the Reggae Girlz's story, think about what drives you. Will you be like the Reggae Girlz and be driven and determined to win no matter the cost? Will you push with all your might? Will you use your undying passion to make your dreams come true, just like they did? If you are ever in a situation where you seem to be the underdog, remember the Reggae Girlz and give it everything you've got. You might end up being just as victorious as they were!

FACTS

1. Soccer is known as the "Beautiful Game." The soccer legend Pelé gave it this name.

2. Studies have shown that teams playing at home tend to have a slight advantage over visiting teams, attributed to crowd support and familiarity with the stadium.

3. Soccer can be played both indoors and outdoors. Indoor soccer is played in gyms or sports halls and is a fun way to play during winter.

4. A hat-trick happens when a player scores three goals in a single match. The term was borrowed from cricket, and it's an outstanding achievement for the player.

5. The ball used in the first World Cup final in 1930 was so heavy that it often deflated during the game.

CHAPTER 11

FIGHT, LADIES, FIGHT

So, you know when you do everything right and are still unhappy about how things turned out? You followed all the steps but still feel bad about it because something still feels off. Of course, this is one of life's biggest disappointments, and sadly, we all know what it feels like. The ladies worldwide who love and play soccer understand how you feel; they've been playing on a bumpy pitch for some time. Many have fought and are still fighting to ensure that soccer is a fun, fair, and inclusive sport for all athletes. If you think about it another way, let's say you're a younger sibling who hates it when the older sibling gets to do what they want. Do you whine and get upset when you get stuck with a lemon (the things you don't want)? Or do you make lemonade like the ladies of FC Barcelona Femeni did?

After years of existing in the shadows of male soccer teams around the country and having no choice but to survive with a small budget, the women's team from Spain held their heads high and juggled school or work around evening practice sessions. To everyone's surprise (everyone but the team, that is—they knew what they could accomplish), the team kept growing and reaching new heights—becoming an inspirational story about determination and dedication.

Remember that budget that I mentioned earlier? The team had a hard choice in front of them; they finally received enough money to make bigger and better choices. Did they want to buy players and enjoy a few years of success? Or would they build from the ground up?

After some thought, they chose a building approach because they could prioritize and focus on nurturing player development. The club grew quickly. At first, they started with the main roster and quickly branched off into minor and youth divisions. They quickly realized that their futures would be brighter if they focused on fostering young talent and creating a system that created skilled players. These players became known throughout women's soccer as masters of creating and controlling plays. Before long, they were considered to be an unstoppable force! Go, FC Barcelona go!

With passion and drive, FC Barcelona has lit a fire that continues spreading, promoting a sense of solidarity among ladies around the country. During a recent World Cup event, it wasn't hard for fans to get swept up in the waves of energy and enthusiasm. The players on the field could finally shine their lights to inspire young girls and women (and even boys and men) with their passion, strength, courage, and dedication. In the years to come, the chances for growth are massive.

So, let's not forget that we, too, are free from limits when we choose to break down barriers, work together, and lead by example. Keeping the leadership fire burning and propelling women's soccer forward, who's next?

Winger (forward) Megan Rapinoe has soared throughout her career, inspiring the USA women's soccer team and fans for years. Have you ever seen her goal celebration? It's bold, as bold as the colors she's dyed her hair with—she plants her feet, legs spread wide, stretching her arms wide, and the best part, the huge, delighted grin across her face as she throws her head back. It looks like she's ready to take off, and in a way, she has. As a player, Megan is constantly evolving, tackling more responsibility, challenging herself to be more accountable, and emotionally invested on or off the pitch. Fans have watched her grow, bounce back, and push past disappointing losses. How does she do it? She says it helps when she remembers that losses are part of the game, and she works on packing up her emotions and pivots to focus on the next day and the next game.

Now, it's your turn. Think of ways to help you keep your spirits high when dealing with a rough patch. Remember, just like Megan, you can't always win or be at your best, but you can control your outlook. A positive outlook will make solving problems easier.

CHAPTER 12

DELIBERATE OWN GOALS EQUALS VICTORY!

As any soccer fan would likely tell you, one of the biggest soccer "sins" is committing an own goal. Nothing is worse than the sadness that settles over the players and the fans after witnessing a player scoring own goals. Now, imagine willingly doing this, but to win!

Let's take it back to 1994 and the tale of the pitch. Two teams, Grenada and Barbados. Their goal is to win, and how will they do that? By scoring on their own net! Wait a minute, isn't that wrong? Yes! Usually, you defend your own net, not your opponents! Well, this game was on a whole other level. Each team had a goal, and the question was. Who would make it to the finals?

Both teams had dreams of winning and qualifying for the finals of the Shell Caribbean Cup tournament (CONCACAF Caribbean Cup). History was in the making; this game would become one of the most entertaining events this tournament would ever see!

Barbados quickly set the pace by scoring two goals to grab the lead. Knowing the stakes were high, Grenada managed to claw back and scored their first goal with about seven minutes left.

Still confused, aren't you? No. Good! You're probably thinking, "This doesn't seem odd, just a regular soccer game." It would have been, except the tournament was played with the golden goal rule. The golden goal rule means that when the teams go into extra time, the first team to score wins. This golden goal was special, though, because it counted as two goals!

One ambitious Barbadian player realized he needed the perfect defensive strategy to stop Grenada from winning. He realized he needed to execute a plan to push both teams into overtime. So, this player did the unthinkable.

Can you guess what he did? Well, he launched the ball past his own keeper and tied the game.

His keeper was stunned, the Grenadians were stunned, and the fans were stunned. This is the one thing that no one thought would have happened, yet it did! There was chaos throughout the stadium!

Grenada quickly recovered and tried as hard as possible to prevent extra time. The only way to do that was to score! Off they went, trying to score a goal into either net, but to other disappointment, the Barbadian players split up and started defending both nets!

Have you ever heard of the old expression, "Turnabout is fair play"? It just means that Grenada was desperate, and they felt they had no choice but to copy the other team to end their misery and head to the showers. (Doing to themselves what Barbados chose not to do, the "turnabout.")

But no such luck; they failed at losing on purpose because Barbados wasn't fooled and realized what Grenada was planning, and split up so they could defend both goals.

The antics didn't stop, and the poor Grenadian team was pretty confused. It took them a moment to realize they could beat Barbados by scoring on their keeper. Yes, it's another own-goal attempt. It seems that maybe everyone "forgot" why they were playing the game, and they were too focused on the golden goal versus playing in the true spirit of the game. What was going on with everyone that day?! So, as they ran back towards their keeper, Barbados kept up the defensive pressure and held off the Grenadians.

And then it was extra time!

And would you believe that only four minutes into extra time, Barbados scored and headed to the finals?

Unsurprisingly, when it was all said and done, the Grenadians were pretty disappointed, and the team's manager commented about the havoc the funny business caused. He went on to say that he felt cheated and that all the confusion wasn't necessary because, in soccer, one should be scoring against one's opponents and not scoring for them (to help yourself win).

Creativity and developing new ideas are captivating and magical experiences. However, you should always remember to consider if your ideas cause harm or are fair and honorable. Decide how to balance different responsibilities in ways that benefit (you and) others. Being adaptable, creative, and thinking outside the box is great when navigating random situations, but it should never stop you from following rules. You should never have to part with your integrity for victory because only truthfully earned victory can be genuinely celebrated!

CHAPTER 13

IT'S A GOAL. NOPE. IT'S A UFO!

Soccer, science, and the story about how ten thousand fans got a shock they didn't expect while watching a game between local rivals Fiorentina and Pistoiese. Just after half-time, the stadium suddenly went quiet. Everyone was speechless as they tried to figure out if this game would become something more than they bargained for. They watched as the game transformed into something more than meets the eye and not what they expected to see.

When you are at a soccer game in Tuscany, what do you expect to see when you look up? Yes, the blue sky, white puffy clouds, the usual. But on this day, if you gazed back down towards the field, you'd notice something odd. Puzzled, you might look around, wondering if anyone else is seeing what you're seeing. Does anyone else see what you're seeing?

You look back up as others also start talking about the strange object. Some people think it's a meteor. Others think it's a fireball. Maybe it's angry soccer gods messing with everyone to force a better match. An idea struck someone in the crowd, and soon, the rumor spread that it was a UFO. People in the crowd nodded in agreement; that had to be it! Superstitions are funny things; they're hard to understand,

Everyone stared, trying to figure out what that white cottony cloud was hanging, no, hovering in the air. Some wondered if they were spiderwebs. Hovering spiderwebs sound like they belong in a horror film, not the soccer field!

Whoever you asked had a different memory of what happened that day. Many dismissed the UFO sightings almost immediately. UFOs aren't real! Instead, they decided to examine nature's clues, as it was fall. What typically migrated, and what was the weather like around this time of year? Most people decided it could be 'angel hair,' something to do with the thousands of spiders that typically migrate around late October.

Did the so-called 'UFO invasion' help the match? Probably not, but let's see if they figured out what was happening.

Players on the field remember seeing what looked like slow-moving glittery silver spheres or egg-like shapes, and fans in the stands described the shapes as fast-moving tubular shapes that stopped and started abruptly.

It would be easy to ignore these 'make-believe' stories if they only happened at the stadium, but that wasn't the case. Witnesses from other parts of Tuscany and nearby towns reported additional UFO sightings that occurred later that day and the following day. Other people described a shining bright light that cast a northern city in an angelic glow.

Speaking of angels, journalists investigating the sightings noticed 'angel hair,' a sticky substance similar to cobwebs or cotton falling from the sky. Samples were collected, and unsurprisingly, like the not entirely unrelated substance called cotton candy, the sticky substance supposedly evaporated before scientists had time to analyze it properly. Did it evaporate? It's a sticky, unsolved mystery for the history books.

According to some reports, the webby stuff contained calcium, silicon, and magnesium. This discovery left many to decide that spiders were to blame for the angel hair, while Italy's National UFO Centre believes it was a magical, supernatural event. Which theory do you believe?

We often face moments that seem puzzling and hard to understand; things happen that don't follow logic or reason. Sometimes, we should embrace the unknown with curiosity instead of ignoring it—you'd be surprised to discover that the unknown is just a sign. It is a way to motivate you to dig deeper to discover more. Believing in myths can be a way to learn and be inspired. Those who are open-minded and eager to learn more about things they might not understand get to explore the world's most interesting things. Therefore, say yes to learning about the questions that nature might throw our way!

CHAPTER 14

EURO-DERELLA

The expression getting more than what you bargained for is something we all hope for. Little unexpected surprises can definitely light up our days. The Denmark team got to experience an unexpected delight. Imagine getting into a tournament you didn't qualify for. Woo-hoo! A screamer—internal pandemonium and excitement are at the top of your to-do list, followed by preparing for the game.

Here's a little backstory.

Unfortunately, Yugoslavia (now known as the countries Serbia and Montenegro) had urgent matters to deal with and decided to pull out of the competition, leaving their spot up for grabs. The second-place team, Denmark, was granted a place in the finals two weeks before the Euro started. Imagine hearing the news that you are going to the finals. Would you be jumping for joy or be filled with nerves? It is fair to say that the players of the Denmark team experienced both of these emotions!

At first, finding the "glass slipper" was a fairytale moment. However, it didn't take long before excitement was quickly replaced with more questions; their competition would be brutal. Denmark would have to play against and beat the likes of England, Sweden, Germany, and France to win the finals, the never-to-be-called-again prince-charmin-pionship.

Hopes were fading as it looked like the pumpkin would appear at midnight after all. Denmark didn't have a good start; they played to a draw against England, and in the next game, they were defeated by their rivals, Sweden. Things started to turn around; fate, at last, was showing kindness.

Denmark must have wished upon many stars because the soccer gods were in a giving mood. As the tournament continued, Denmark began winning, first beating France to advance to the semis. Then, in the next round, they won against the Netherlands on penalty kicks and completed the upset by winning in the finals against Germany.

The story of Denmark's victory in the Euro is an excellent example of how life can be unpredictable and full of jaw-dropping moments. From planning for the next Euro in four years to pivoting to playing in the current tournament, Denmark had the odds stacked against them. Despite setbacks, Denmark pushed forward with determination, defeating their competition and raising the trophy in the finals. Determination isn't just about ignoring challenges; it's about welcoming the idea that failure can prepare you to make your grand comeback. Denmark's run to glory teaches us there is no limit to what we can achieve when we don't allow ourselves to be overwhelmed by defeat or frustration. How will you use Denmark's spirit of commitment to guide you on your quest?

Let's be motivated by Denmark's fairytale and historic win. Let us be inspired and believe we can accomplish incredible things when we approach challenges enthusiastically and with determination. Like players on the pitch who strive to be alert, we should, in life, be ready to react to any unexpected challenges that come our way. This ability to predict and react positively to the unknown can open doors that may have been closed or hidden away.

What do we want to see when we look into the mirror on the wall? I hope you want to see your triumphs and gain confidence in discovering the best plays to help you win life's championships. But remember, wishing isn't enough. It's about finding the sunshine on cloudy days. Sometimes, you must make the wrong turns; sometimes, you must miss opportunities to find your true path. There are also times you should grab an opportunity with both hands because it can lead to great victory! We must make good choices in life. However, when we fail to do so, accepting the past for what it is and focusing on the future is an excellent life skill to have.

CHAPTER 15

OH CANADA!

Welcome to our next chapter. I wanted to share a few amazing moments from the Canadian men's and women's soccer teams with you.

Are you ready to enjoy a good time? It's a tale that's not too long; it's just that Canada deserves to shine a little on this day. Canadian soccer teams are making headlines for their impressive performances, wowing their legions of fans. Move over Canadian football, baseball, and hockey; soccer wants a moment!

Did you know the men's national team has twice qualified for the World Cup? The women's team has a long and magnificent record; they've won multiple international competitions and recently won gold at the Olympics. It is clear that the Canadian ladies know what they are doing!

On the grand stage, during big games, top players like Christine Sinclair showcased her dominance; during that World Cup tournament, she scored 11 goals, including five in one game. These performances crowned her as the tournament MVP. Another Canadian rising talent from the Canadian men's team is Alphonso Davies—you better start paying close attention to this soccer whiz. Davies is only in his early 20s, but his skillful plays during a recent World Cup game made history. Davies scored the Canadian men's first-ever goal at a World Cup only 68 seconds into the match—the historic goal redeeming him for missing an earlier penalty kick during Canada's opening loss to Belgium.

Have you ever heard of finesse? It is a special quality that makes your ideas just that much better. Finesse means doing things skillfully, gracefully, with guts and charm. If you've been watching the Canadian soccer teams rise, haven't you noticed how they have dazzled the world and shown what determination, heart, and finesse look like? Take a look at your favorite teams. What qualities do they share? What qualities are different? Now, take a look at yourself. When you genuinely care about something, are you willing to fight for it with determination and finesse?

When you focus on finesse, you'll notice that you can turn a disappointing day into something fantastic and memorable. Here are a few examples of what I mean. It's like when you're playing with your friends; finesse could be when you remember that if your friend looks to the left, he will kick to the right. With that knowledge, you could position yourself to block the shot. It's identifying what details matter the most, followed by thinking quickly to decide what moves (or skills) you'll act on first.

Finesse is also about being creative and using your imagination. When you apply finesse creatively, you'll notice details that didn't stand out to you the first time. It's like noticing these details and making simple changes creates beauty. In this example, you can think of finesse like being super focused when painting or drawing. You realize you're spending more time than usual to ensure the water is the right shade of blue and the lines for the ripples are not too long or too short. That's finesse. It's paying attention to the small details to create the idea you were thinking of. When we really focus on the things that matter to us, we see ourselves becoming stronger and growing at an amazing pace. Staying passionate and focused is the best thing we can do as we play the game of life.

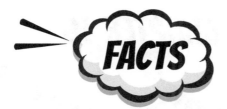

FACTS

1. The bicycle kick is a spectacular soccer move where a player kicks the ball while in midair, often resulting in stunning goals.

2. The Golden Boot is awarded to the top goalscorer of the FIFA World Cup, recognizing their exceptional performance on the world stage. Lionel Messi has won the award six times, the most out of every winner!

3. A red card in soccer signifies a player's dismissal from the game due to serious foul play or misconduct, often resulting in their team playing with one fewer player.

4. Soccer has the power to unite people across cultures, languages, and backgrounds, showcasing the universal appeal of the sport.

5. Cristiano Ronaldo's iconic "¡Siiii!" celebration, where he jumps, spins, and shouts, is famous worldwide. It even became a famous meme!}

CHAPTER 16

WHEN THE STUFF OF DREAMS, AKA THE FOOD OF THE GODS, IS BAD

What gives us a roller coaster of emotions more than watching a team, our team, waffling back and forth? Battling our emotions, we're super happy one moment and super sad the next. Our emotions can't handle this much drama, can they? Imagine you're watching a brilliant defensive game; both teams are going back and forth, save after brilliant save, timely and well-executed dribbles, players taking shots at the goal—and finally, a goal! Yes, and hooray, and while you're celebrating—the other team scores. Oof, what a drag.

Now imagine your team losing an important game, partly because most of them have a tummy ache. Of course, no one is perfect, and we all have days when we just don't feel our best. Will you be understanding towards a teammate if they cost you the game?

A tummy ache costs a team a game. Yes! What has lasagna done to you lately? Hopefully, it's been nothing more than a yummy meal you had for dinner. It has been? That's great. Glad to hear it!

Unfortunately for the Spurs, lasagna wasn't as kind to them. So, let's talk about what happened to this poor team. The Spurs had qualifying on their minds; they needed one win to make it into the Champions League. It was the last day of the season, a day they'd been waiting for. It's safe to say they were probably pretty excited, wouldn't you be? You can imagine how close you are to finally realizing your dreams.

Anyway, the Spurs are the visiting team set to play West Ham, and they decided to stay at a local hotel. Not wanting to go out to eat, the players chose to stay at the hotel and make a beeline straight for the buffet—where they could pick chicken, pasta, steak, or lasagna. It was a great meal and a great time laughing and joking with teammates before heading to bed.

Early the next day, the team doctor kept getting phone call after phone call after phone call. Nearly ten or so players had woken up feeling sick. Now, if you think it is hard to make up a soccer team when you have ten players down, you'd be right! Talk about challenging numbers!

Everyone has experienced a time when they felt sick but still had to find a way to manage attending school or an important event. You can imagine how worried those players must have been, hours away from a big game they're too sick to play in. The Spurs tried to get permission to delay the game but had no luck, so they started scrambling to find solutions. First, they started calling in substitutes, but they soon realized that there weren't enough and that some of the sick players had to play on the pitch. Imagine how low the morale was. Players who were usually filled with nervous energy were now filled with worry, looking pale and sick—it was probably an odd sight. Imagine if you were one of those players. Would you be brave enough to step out onto the field if your stomach was unsettled?

Even though they weren't feeling their best, the players knew they had to try as hard as possible to be positive and upbeat. It was getting closer to game time, and some players did their best to boost morale, secretly hoping it would be enough to spark the other players to dig deep and pull off a miraculous win. What a special moment that would be! Sure, it was challenging, but the Spurs tried their best to rally together and push through. But they couldn't pull off the upset (tummy) win. Sadly, they lost the game. While the players must have been disappointed in their loss, they had become closer to each other through their shared suffering. They had really come together as a team, trying their best to stand strong even in tough times. That is what team sports are all about, and while they didn't get a victory that day, they found strength in their team!

So, let's talk about grit, which is a fancy word for never giving up. In soccer and life, grit is essential. It takes effort and hard work; you could be focused on making your favorite meals, studying for a big test, or playing soccer. You must practice, make mistakes, and ultimately, push and encourage yourself or your team. Building character to balance strengths and weaknesses is vital. When you have grit, you never give up. You keep practicing, keep working hard, and keep trying your best.

But sometimes, people don't have grit. Maybe they have doubts—luckily, it's not as dramatic as getting sick before the last game of the season! Even when it seems like giving up is the easiest thing to do, please don't do it. That's not you. When you give up too easily, you miss out on all the good things that come with grit—having it gives you chances to be open to embrace possibility. Often, we are afraid of what might happen when we fail. We become so afraid of the prospect of failure that we don't take the time to consider what would happen if we were victorious!

CHAPTER 17

MESSI, PENALTIES, AND MISSES

Penalty kicks are challenging to execute because the other team's goalkeeper is focused on keeping the ball out of the net; it's the ultimate matchup. Would it be a victory or a humbling loss? Will the kick be true? Or will the gloved hand make the stop?

Penalty kicks are a fascinating part of soccer, and it's a nail-biter when the final score depends on them! There are several things to consider when it comes to a successful penalty kick. The player needs to have the skill and ability to keep calm. Fatigue or injury can affect the player's ability to take the shot or make the save. The weather or time of day can also play a role, and then there's all the guessing involved. The player taking the shot has to guess which way the goalie will jump, and the goalie has to guess what direction the ball may go in. Or, the player may try using trick shots, hoping that they'll force the goalie to dive the wrong way. It's not just a simple kick anymore, is it?

Lionel Messi's phenomenal performances on the field are fun. His popularity is hard to ignore! Many think he's one of the best players ever! He's won many awards and had several high-profile championship runs. Fans love his gifted and magical left foot!

Messi is an amazing player, and while he has his faults, he's trying to work through them. He doesn't have a handle on converting penalties, much to the disappointment of his fans. Oh gosh, you can imagine it might drive Messi crazy! I'm sure he realized that something had to change, and he must have practiced and practiced.

Practice isn't making perfect, not yet, anyway.

Unfortunately, Messi is still working on perfecting his penalty kicks. In 2016, Messi had a chance to win the game for Argentina with a penalty kick.

But. He. Missed. Imagine his disappointment.

After that game, Messi had to ignore many negative comments. His doubters claimed he wasn't as good as they thought and questioned his ability to perform under pressure. Messi didn't let the negativity get to him. What did he do? He practiced, and soon, Messi proved that he could score on penalty kicks; he ended the unlucky streak during a crucial qualifying match against Ecuador!

What can we learn from Messi's story? We can learn that thriving when facing challenges is more than thinking about only winning or losing. It's about believing in ourselves, never giving up, even when facing barriers, and finding the strength to bounce back from failure and try again.

Have you ever faced a challenge that seemed too big and too powerful? Did you ask for help, or did you figure it out alone? Maybe it was a test you didn't study for, you were working with other kids you hadn't worked with before, or you stood up for yourself. Whatever the roadblock was, you had to overcome the feeling of wanting to give up. Success finds and motivates people committed to trying again and working through their problems, building a legacy of triumph.

CHAPTER 18

TOP SCORE(RS)!

Should we talk about Messi again? Maybe we will! This chapter is about all-time top scorers—keep reading to see if Messi makes another appearance. After all, there are so many top scorers to unpack and so many top guys to show! I've decided on the following guys. Whether or not that's the right decision, I'll leave that to you. Maybe you'll look up how many goals your favorite top scorer has.

Are you tired of waiting? Well, here we go!

He scored 757 goals, he's one of the greats. Winning three World Cups, he's an icon. Yes, I'm talking about Pele. Always blowin' his own horn, he's exaggerated his record once or twice, and according to him, he's scored over 1000 goals. Unofficially, if you look hard enough, you may find he has nearly 1300. It makes you wonder what happened. Why don't those goals count? Why are they unofficial goals? Was it poor record-keeping, or did some competitions not count? Pele was powerful and so lovingly adored worldwide that a country announced a temporary truce to enjoy his incredible skills on the pitch.

In 1969, after Pele scored (unofficially) what was at the time his 1000th goal, the fans ran onto the field to celebrate, stopping the game for almost 30 minutes so that they could honor Pele by carrying him around. Ole! Ole! Ole! Ole! Did you know that every year, Brazilians celebrate November 19th, Pele Day?

Now, the time has come to move on to one of the best strikers in soccer today. You'll notice a year or two where he is the only player who outscored Cristiano Ronaldo and Lionel Messi in yearly top-scoring rankings. Say hello to a player with an uncanny ability to score a goal every one and a half to two games, Luis Suarez. He has an honorary mention in our top scorer chapter with over 500 goals and counting under his boots.

You knew he would be back, right? Yes, Messi again—to be fair, I can't mention top scorers without Lionel Messi. Don't worry; this will be short and sweet. Since Messi started in 2003, he has booted in at least 819 goals. This next fact has nothing to do with goals, but since we're talking numbers, Messi has a social media post celebrating his 2022 World Cup victory with nearly 80 million likes!

Last up, how about Portugal's own Cristiano Ronaldo? Cristiano has what it takes to be this chapter's hot topic: top goal scorer. For the fifth time in his career, he recently finished as the year's top goal scorer with 54 goals. But wait, there's more: Cristiano added another monumental record to his arsenal by ending the 60-year reign of former all-time top scorer Josef Bican. Cristiano is sitting in the top spot with over 870 goals. Isn't that impressive? Who knows how many goals Cristiano will have when he retires? Maybe he'll hit 1000!

Do you know what prowess means? It's when you believe in the power of harmony. Harmony is not just about individuals working together; it's about finding balance in everything you do. It's about making sure things line up the way they should—think stacking Jenga pieces so they don't fall or the feeling you get when you get enough points to buy a new skill or emote in a videogame. It's about thinking ahead and correctly guessing what someone else may need by recognizing and considering others' emotions.

You can enjoy harmony like you enjoy the feeling you get when you master a new skill. Do you apply what you've learned to solve other problems? Do you look for ways to improve? Mastering new skills allows you to be in control and guides you so that you can avoid and get past obstacles. So, keep practicing, keep learning, and never give up! As we grow and change, we pick up new skills to develop. These skills are ways to connect with others, boost our self-confidence, and even lead us to our future jobs. That is why being open to new things and embracing the unfamiliar is important!

CHAPTER 19

THE HAND OF GOD GOAL

What if he made a deal with God? Tell me, what if this player could make a deal to give Argentina the win? Maybe he made a deal to get the world not to pay attention to where his hand was placed. The deal was to give the world an experience that would live on forever!

So come on, put your hands together, bow your head, and say a little prayer.

All done!

So, to repeat, the deal was to make sure no one was paying attention to his hand.

Look, world. What hands? Now, speaking of soccer and its rules, you know players are only supposed to use their feet unless they're the keeper, right?

What a story, the more I think about it. Maybe God did swap places; maybe he was running up and down that pitch. Maybe he decided this game was the perfect time to answer a few prayers. It was time to grant some grace. If you don't believe me, then after you're finished reading this, go and take a few moments to watch that goal—it was something!

Nothing is more divine than a miracle—when your superstitions become granted wishes. The Argentine team depended on Diego Maradona to deliver miracles; on this day, it would be no different.

During the 1986 World Cup tournament, Maradona kept turning doubt into hope, hope into joy, and joy turned into what you may now know as the 'Hand of God' goal. He welcomed the responsibility of carrying the hopes and dreams of his country on his shoulders. Maradona knew that the world outside of the pitch wasn't in a good place. He used a discouraging time for inspiration, a powerful one to motivate his teammates and keep their spirits up. Maradona led by example. He was positive, and soon enough, so were they! Focused on winning the championship, England was in their way, but nothing could stop them.

Then, the goal. Argentina was up 1-0.

On the other side of that goal was the side that God wasn't happy with, the English side. But why? What did they do wrong? More often than I can say, England has had their fair share of being unlucky. And winning in do-or-die situations? Count them out!

You can imagine the English players noticed God-Maradona's hand punching the ball into the net—that wasn't a header, not even close!

There was no whistle, so the goal counted (and video replay didn't exist back then). England, with several superstitions of their own, must have thought they were coldly being served revenge. How could the referees have missed the obvious hand ball? They doubted the referee's view was blocked, and they were disappointed. Poor England, to be the victim of a legendary goal.

After the game, what happened? Nothing much! It was another day, another legendary performance, where Maradona rose to the occasion. It was a header, according to him, and he described the famous goal as using a bit of his head and having a little push from the hand of God.

One more thing: it wasn't only the 'Hand of God' that ruined England's dreams. Nope, that first goal wasn't what sealed England's fate. Sadly, sometimes fate works in mysterious ways. England's confidence was shattered because it only took four minutes for Maradona to get the ball again, zipping by three defenders and scoring again! Game over!

Maradona's story shows us that luck (God) and being imaginative can help us get more chances and opportunities. It's like saying to look both ways before crossing the street, think before you talk, and always be kind to others, the golden rules! Imagination can be about making the most of what you have and turning challenges into opportunities. So, let's get started! Give yourself an advantage. Even when you don't have the hand of God to guide you, be your driving force. You are in charge of your destiny, so take the lead and try your best to make the most of the opportunities that come your way.

CHAPTER 20

SHAME ON YOU, ANTI-DIBU

In an oof heard worldwide—a goalkeeper has to find a new bag of tricks to get a one-up during a penalty kick. He can no longer taunt during penalties, even though all he did was stop the shots he needed to stop. Are you saying he can't move around?

So, does this mean that the players get to run back on a 45-degree angle for a few feet and kick the ball? If they whiff, that's it? No more fancy foot fake-outs? Ugh, that would make penalty kicks so boring. But here we are!

Let's talk about rules. Rules can and do change. It just seems like the rules are changing to keep a good keeper down. Argentine keeper Emiliano 'Dibu" Martínez has been unhappy about the new soccer rule unofficially known as the 'anti-Dibu law.'

What is this new rule? It limits what keepers can do during penalty shootouts.

Say goodbye, fun. No more swag surfing. No more distractions, no more Kelce-Swifty-ness to confuse the players so they will mess up their kicks and miss the net. Very unfair and anti-fun.

Speaking of fun, Dibu shone in the 2022 Qatar World Cup. His talent for distracting his opponents and preventing them from making proper shot attempts earned him plenty of adoring fans in his home country of Argentina and worldwide.

Back to this rule that will dim the talents that have been on full display for some time—the 'anti-Dibu law' says that the keeper can't fidget or move in a way that could distract the kicker in an 'illegal' way. What does that mean?

Glad you asked. It's things like touching the net, the posts, or jumping up and touching the crossbar.

Doesn't it seem like the new rules will help the kickers?

I'm sure it does! No new rules for them! It looks like they're still allowed to do 'power-ups' and special distraction-style moves.

Why did the league change the rules? Well, let me share a famous Dibu stunt.

Dibu also plays for Aston Villa. During a game, he rushed out of position to 'request' that a Manchester United midfielder give his penalty to Cristiano Ronaldo so that they would have a better chance of scoring.

Ouch!

Being bold, a force that transforms the world around you, can greatly boost your ego because everyone recognizes your brilliance. But it can also be a pain because if you're too good at something, the rules may change in what you may think is an attempt to hold you back.

Don't look at it that way. Our approach to situations makes all the difference.

Remember that when people can't do what you do, they may want to change the rules or not want to hang out with you as often as they used to. But that means you may have to dig deeper and find new ways to exceed expectations and limitations. If you think about it, Dibu's historic win with Argentina in the Copa America wasn't just about antics in front of the goal. It was a celebration of hard work and determination.

Use your inner Dibu, not your anti-Dibu. Be open and willing to find ways to unlock your full potential.

Running low on inspiration? Breathe! Now, think about it. Do you think Dibu thought his antics would cause the rules to be changed? Of course not! But he isn't letting change stop him, so the same goes for you. No one can deny that life isn't always easy. In fact, sometimes, it can be quite challenging! Even when we expect that things will go smoothly, we can be surprised. However, how we react to challenges and obstacles makes all the difference. It can divide the winners from the rest.

1. Lionel Messi used to suffer from growth hormone deficiency and needed expensive treatment as a child.

2. Soccer is played on every continent, including Antarctica. Scientists and support staff stationed at research stations there often organize matches to pass the time during the long months of isolation.

3. The sport of soccer is over 2,000 years old, with ancient civilizations like the Greeks, Romans, and Chinese all playing early versions of the game!

4. The World Cup trophy, awarded to the winning team, weighs around 13.5 pounds and is made of solid 18-carat gold.

5. The fastest red card in soccer history was given just 2 seconds into a game – talk about a record-breaking start!

CONCLUSION

What a fantastic journey through the world of soccer! Each story has shown us that passion and determination can lead to greatness regardless of background or circumstance.

Through victories and defeats, the stories taught us the importance of resilience and teamwork, reminding us that success is not just about individual skill but also about lifting each other up and working together towards a common goal.

We learned about the transformative power of unity and camaraderie through the heartwarming tale of a devoted soccer fan who was granted a cherished moment to relive the stadium's atmosphere. We have witnessed the sportsmanship of jersey swapping at the end of every game, a sign of affection and respect. Not only that, but we have laughed at the crazy superstitions that players have. What wonderful story will yours be? Whatever it is, be a star on and off the field, and remember always to be yourself!

So, whether you're kicking a ball on a neighborhood field or cheering from the sidelines, always remember the lessons learned from these remarkable players and inspiring stories. Let them fuel your own journey and inspire you to reach for the stars.

REFERENCES

Alabama FC and Birmingham United Soccer Association. *Interesting Fun Soccer Facts.* (2023, February 4). . https://www.birminghamunited.com/funfacts/

Ang, E. (2022, December 30). *Football: 10 things about the legend Pele.* The Straits Times. https://www.straitstimes.com/sport/football-10-things-about-the-legend-pele

AStv. (2016, April 22). *10 years since one of football's funniest ever own goals.* Diario AS. https://en.as.com/en/2016/04/23/soccer/1461363041_489354.html

Atzenhoffer, T. (2012, July 4). *Top 10 Soccer Superstitions.* Bleacher Report. https://bleacherreport.com/articles/1243400-top-10-soccer-superstitions

Bailey, R. (2014, October 17). *10 Matches with a Shocking Amount of Red Cards.* Bleacher Report. https://bleacherreport.com/articles/2235142-10-matches-with-a-shocking-amount-of-red-cards

Bandini, N., & Ashdown, J. (2009, April 1). *Has a referee ever been sent off?* The Guardian. https://www.theguardian.com/football/2009/apr/01/referee-sent-off-footballers-honoured-the-knowledge#:~:text=%22I%20was%20once%20involved%20in

Baxter, K. (2021, December 24). *Peace for a day: How soccer brought a brief truce to World War I on Christmas Day 1914.* Los Angeles Times. https://www.latimes.com/sports/soccer/story/2021-12-24/christmas-truce-soccer-world-war-germany-britain-adolf-hitler

Beard, A. (2020, July 1). *Life's Work: An Interview with Megan Rapinoe.* Harvard Business Review. https://hbr.org/2020/07/lifes-work-an-interview-with-megan-rapinoe#:~:text=An%20outspoken%20advocate%20for%20LGBTQ

Bonn, K. (2022, November 30). *Messi World Cup penalty miss: Argentina star shot saved by Szczesny, but how often does it happen?* The Sporting News. https://www.sportingnews.com/ca/soccer/news/messi-penalty-miss-world-cup-argentina-save-szczesny/qpzskjcqbg0kkzoqmkseqhrg

Boon, J. (2018, February 2). *OFF YOU GO! The birth of red cards: How English football was inspired by traffic lights to give players their marching orders* The Sun. https://www.thesun.co.uk/sport/football/5483338/red-yellow-card-history-george-best-ken-aston/

Brennan, F. (2023, July 19). *Most goals scored in a soccer game: Did Bayern Munich reach record with 27-0 preseason friendly win?* The Sporting News. https://www.sportingnews.com/ca/soccer/news/most-goals-scored-soccer-game-record/ys0xo8uegzcvo6ryhboyy7n8

Brischetto, P. (2022, December 18). *Lionel Messi penalty kick history: Argentina captain's record on penalties*. The Sporting News. https://www.sportingnews.com/ca/soccer/news/lionel-messi-penalty-history-record-argentina/wm5uvkvdpi4bp85trqxvsbom

Burnton, S. (2018, March 29). *When extra time had no end: how one match lasted 3hrs and 23mins*. The Guardian. https://www.theguardian.com/football/2018/mar/29/extra-time-no-end-worlds-longest-match-stockport-doncaster

Cardenas, F. (2022, May 16). .*The origins of the Hand of God, a goal still contentious two years after Maradona's death*. The Athletic. https://theathletic.com/3984530/2022/12/16/hand-of-god-maradona-world-cup/

Chakraborty, S. (2022, August 31). *Five players who have missed the most penalties in the 21st century*. Sportskeeda. https://www.sportskeeda.com/football/5-players-missed-penalties-21st-century-totti-ibrahimovic

Cooper, B., & Abbott, M. (2020, May 21). *Why Nottingham Forest fans sing Mull of Kintyre and when it started*. Nottinghamshire Live. https://www.nottinghampost.com/sport/football/nottingham-forest-mull-of-kintyre-2410393

Cords, S. (2018, June 22). *Superstitions on the soccer pitch*. Dw.com. https://www.dw.com/en/superstitious-soccer-weird-rituals-on-the-football-pitch/a-44287460

Corrigan, D. (2020, September 24). *13 trophies and 198 goals - but was Luis Suarez underappreciated at Barcelona?* The Athletic. https://theathletic.com/2081659/2020/09/24/luis-suarez-barcelona-transfer-atletico-la-liga/

Cunningham, J. (2019). *Why Do Some People Call Football "Soccer"?* Encyclopaedia Britannica. https://www.britannica.com/story/why-do-some-people-call-football-soccer

Dixon, R. (2023). *How Team Canada became "the best story in World Cup qualifying."* Sportsnet. https://www.sportsnet.ca/soccer/longform/how-team-canada-became-the-best-story-in-world-cup-qualifying/

Eccleshare, C. (2022, May 19). *Tottenham's Champions League push, Lasagne-gate and how protocols will stop it happening again*. The Athletic. https://theathletic.com/3319307/2022/05/19/tottenham-lasagne-champions-league/

ESPN News Services. (2023, December 30). *Ronaldo to end 2023 as world's top goal scorer*. ESPN. https://www.espn.com/soccer/story/_/id/39211354/cristiano-ronaldo-end-2023-world-top-goalscorer

Everybody Soccer. *Best Moments in Canadian Soccer History*. (2022, December 5). https://everybodysoccer.com/even-the-goalkeepers-like-to/2022/12/5/best-moments-in-canadian-soccer-history

FC Bayern München AG. (2019, April 23). *25th anniversary of Helmer's ghost goal*. FC Barn München. https://fcbayern.com/en/news/2019/04/looking-back-helmers-ghost-goal

FIFA (2024). *The Long Walk: The History of the Penalty Shoot-Out*. https://www.fifa.com/fifaplus/en/articles/the-long-walk-documentary-the-history-of-the-penalty-shoot-out

Fitch, D. (2013, January 19). *Soccer's 8 Greatest Cinderella Stories of All Time*. Bleacher Report. https://bleacherreport.com/articles/1490847-soccers-8-greatest-cinderella-stories-of-all-time

Football, F. (2022, December 26). *Socceroos star Cummings reveals real story behind jersey swap snub and classy Giroud act*. Fox Sports. https://www.foxsports.com.au/football/world-cup/fifa-world-cup-2022-jason-cummings-and-olivier-giroud-shirt-swap-reaction-updates-socceroos-france/news-story/2541a1fbedb366ab2a1f2e0e898dd642

Footballhistory (2014). *The history of football (soccer)*. https://www.footballhistory.org/

Fricker, M. (2024, February 20). *Partially sighted gran, 92, is moved to tears by visit to Nottingham Forest*. The Mirror. https://www.mirror.co.uk/sport/football/news/football-fan-92-ailing-eyesight-32173276

Goal. (2021, June 28). *What is a "ghost goal"? England vs Germany & Liverpool vs Chelsea goal-line incidents*. The Sporting News. https://www.sportingnews.com/ca/soccer/news/what-is-a-ghost-goal-liverpool-vs-chelsea-champions-league-controversy-classic-goal-line-incidents/x0n9doqssgu819dg8b8v6v2yr

Guido. (2008, October 29). *Barbados vs. Grenada in '94: The Most Bizarre Match Ever*. Bleacher Report. https://bleacherreport.com/articles/74831-barbados-vs-grenada-in-94-the-most-bizarre-match-ever

Hampton, B. (2016, March 25). *The 10 Greatest Real Life Football Fairytales Of All Time*. The18. https://the18.com/en/soccer-news/10-greatest-real-life-football-fairytales-all-time

Hoskin, R. (2022, March 27). *Vanuatu 46-0 Micronesia: The incredible story of the world record win*. GiveMeSport. https://www.givemesport.com/87989074-vanuatu-46-0-micronesia-the-incredible-story-of-the-world-record-win/

Hughes, R. (2014, December 23). *Tale of 1914 Christmas Day Truce Is Inspiring, Though Hard to Believe*. The New York Times. https://www.nytimes.com/2014/12/24/sports/soccer/tale-of-1914-christmas-day-truce-soccer-game.html

Jack R., Joy, B., Richard G., Peter A., & Weil, E. (2019). *football | History, Rules, & Significant Players*. Encyclopædia Britannica. https://www.britannica.com/sports/football-soccer

Jobs in Football (2023, May 6). *The Highest Scoring Soccer Games Ever*. https://jobsinfootball.com/blog/highest-scoring-soccer-games-ever/

Jones, R. (2024, February 19). *Lifelong Forest fan who lost eyesight fulfils wish of hearing "Mull of Kintyre."* Independent. https://www.independent.co.uk/tv/sport/nottingham-forest-mull-of-kintyre-b2498865.html

Kelly, R. (2021, February 18). *Football's famous superstitions: Terry's toilet trick, kissing Barthez's head & the game's weirdest rituals*. The Sporting News. https://www.sportingnews.com/ca/uefa-champions-league/list/footballs-famous-superstitions-terrys-toilet-trick-kissing-barthezs-head-weirdest-rituals/5rrqxb9r49eh11drsedo7ieun

Lavacca, K. (2022, December 16). *Pickles the dog was considered a hero after sniffing out the stolen World Cup trophy in 1966*. ABC7 New York. https://abc7ny.com/world-cup-stolen-pickles-the-dog-england/12578563/#:~:text=World%20Cup-

Mabert, T. (2011, November 25). *World Football: 15 Ridiculous Red Cards*. Bleacher Report. https://bleacherreport.com/articles/956309-world-football-15-ridiculous-red-cards

Mackenzie, A., & Pope, C. (2022, March 29). *The 50 most heartbreaking moments in football*. FourFourTwo. https://www.fourfourtwo.com/features/the-50-most-heartbreaking-moments-in-football

Manister, R. (2023, August 2). *Jamaica's "Reggae Girls" overcome long odds to advance in Women's World Cup*. CBS News. https://www.cbsnews.com/news/jamaica-brazil-world-cup-2023-how-the-reggae-girls-beat-odds-to-advance

May, S. (2023, January 24). *Australia star Cummings finally gets Giroud's shirt following World Cup dispute*. TalkSPORT. https://talksport.com/football/1312328/jason-cummings-olivier-giroud-ac-milan-world-cup-australia/

Mboroki, J. (2014, December 24). *A football match came to a halt 60 years ago when spectators spotted unidentified objects flying over a Florence stadium*. Unbelievable Facts. https://unbelievable-facts.com/2014/12/a-football-match-came-to-a-halt-60-years-ago-when-spectators-spotted-unidentified-objects-flying-over-a-florence-stadium.html

Miller, N. (2023, December 25). *The story of the First World War Christmas truce: How much football was actually played?* The Athletic. https://theathletic.com/5155123/2023/12/25/christmas-truce-world-war-one-football/

MLSsoccer Staff. (2022, November 27). *Alphonso Davies scores Canada's first World Cup goal against Croatia*. MLSsoccer. https://www.mlssoccer.com/news/alphonso-davies-scores-canada-s-first-world-cup-goal-against-croatia#:~:text=Alphonso%20Davies%20scores%20Canada

Morgan, R. (2022, November 30). *Lionel Messi makes unwanted World Cup history after 'embarrassing' act*. Yahoo Sport. https://au.sports.yahoo.com/fifa-world-cup-2022-lionel-messi-unwanted-history-joke-act-211517978.html

Murray, S. (2015, December 17). *Shirt swapping: new to NFL, but long part of soccer's rich tradition*. The Guardian. https://www.theguardian.com/football/2015/dec/17/shirt-swapping-nfl-soccer-culture-tradition

Myers, S. (2022, November 29). *Canadian men make soccer history at 2022 World Cup*. University of Calgary. https://ucalgary.ca/news/canadian-men-make-soccer-history-2022-world-cup

Nesci, G. (2012, May 9). *11 Most Heartbreaking Moments in World Football History*. Bleacher Report. https://bleacherreport.com/articles/1177489-11-most-heartbreaking-moments-in-world-football-history

Nuñez, F. R. (2023, August 4). *"Dibu" Martinez on "anti-Dibu" penalty rule: "They did it too late."* Buenos Aires Herald. https://buenosairesherald.com/sports/stars/dibu-martinez/dibu-martinez-on-anti-dibu-penalty-rule-they-did-it-too-late

Nwokolo, C. (2022, March 31). *Top 5 Bald Footballers In The World (2023)*. Top Soccer Blog. https://topsoccerblog.com/top-5-bald-footballers-2020/

OpenGoaaal. (n.d.) *Nine Best Soccer Moves to Trick Defenders.* Retrieved March 6, 2024, from https://opengoaaalusa.com/blogs/news/soccer-moves#:~:text=Some%20 famous%20soccer%20moves%20include

Padula, R. (2014, October 24). *The day UFOs stopped play.* BBC News. https://www.bbc. com/news/magazine-29342407

Perform. (2021, July 9). *Luis Suárez hits 500th career goal - AS.com.* Web.archive.org. https://web.archive.org/web/20210709184944/https://en.as.com/en/2021/03/21/ football/1616356469_129643.html

Pesca, M. (2010, June 16). *Soccer Players Blame Mistakes On Irritating Vuvuzelas.* NPR. https://www.npr.org/sections/showmeyourcleats/2010/06/15/127864984/vuvuzelas-louder-than-chainsaws-but-still-charming

Prosper, I. (2023, August 9). *The Inspirational Story of Jamaica's Women's Football (Soccer) Team.* LinkedIn. https://www.linkedin.com/pulse/inspirational-story-jamaicas-womens-football-soccer-team-ivy-prosper

Sandler, T. (2023, August 9). *5 Fun Facts About Lionel Messi.* Fangirl Sports Network. https:// fgsn.com/5-fun-facts-about-lionel-messi-2/

Simon. (2023). *All the football slang you'll ever need.* GO Blog | EF GO Blog. https://www. ef.com/wwen/blog/language/all-the-football-slang-youll-ever-need/

SI Wire. (2015, July 7). *Watch: USWNT leads crowd in "I believe that we just won" chant.* Sports Illustrated. https://www.si.com/soccer/2015/07/07/uswnt-world-cup-victory-rally-chant-video

Squizzato, D. (2022, November 22). *Top 10 historic moments for Canada's national soccer teams.* Team Canada - Official Olympic Team Website. https://olympic. ca/2022/11/22/top-10-historic-moments-for-canadas-national-soccer-teams/

Stroud, J., & Hepburn, D. (2022, October 9). An 11 of players with most red cards in football history. GiveMeSport. https://www.givemesport.com/most-red-cards-football-history/#:~:text=46%20red%20cards&text=Gerardo%20Bedoya%20holds%20the%20 record

Sweeny, S., Haggerty, T., & Internet Archive. (1997). Wacky soccer facts to kick around. In *Internet Archive.* New York, NY : Sports Illustrated for Kids. https://archive.org/ details/wackysoccerfacts00swee

Szymanski, S. (2022, November 9). *Why Maradona's "Hand of God" goal is priceless -- and unforgettable.* The Conversation. https://theconversation.com/why-maradonas-hand-of-god-goal-is-priceless-and-unforgettable-193760

Tanner, R. (2022, June 21). *The unwritten rules of shirt swapping.* The Athletic. https:// theathletic.com/2899189/2022/06/21/shirt-swapping-football/

Taysom, J. (2020, November 11). *The story behind of Paul McCartney song "Mull of Kintyre" a love letter to Scotland.* Far Out Magazine. https://faroutmagazine.co.uk/paul-mccartney-mull-of-kintyre-song-meaning/#:~:text=The%20uplifting%20message%20 that%20was

Thomas, L. (2023, July 23). *The World Cup and the Frustrating, Inspiring State of Women's Soccer*. The New Yorker. https://www.newyorker.com/sports/sporting-scene/the-world-cup-and-the-frustrating-inspiring-state-of-womens-soccer

Towle, M. (2013, May 8). *10 Most Touching Moments in World Football History*. Bleacher Report. https://bleacherreport.com/articles/1632770-10-most-touching-moments-in-world-football-history

White, M. (2022, November 25). *"I Believe That We Will Win" Cheer Was Born at the Naval Academy*. Coffee or Die Magazine. https://coffeeordie.com/i-believe-that-we-will-win-cheer

Williams, M. (2024, January 5). *Top ten highest goalscorers of all time: Cristiano Ronaldo and World Cup winner Lionel Messi separated by Josef Bican*. TalkSPORT. https://talksport.com/football/691008/highest-goalscorers-ever-ronaldo-messi-josef-bican-pele/

Wikipedia. *Ghost goal*. (2020, June 19). https://en.wikipedia.org/wiki/Ghost_goal

Wilson, J. (2020, May 5). *Lampard's 2010 Ghost Goal and the Video Replay Revolution it Helped Inspire*. Sports Illustrated. https://www.si.com/soccer/2020/05/05/frank-lampard-ghost-goal-south-africa-2010-world-cup-var-technology

Witz, B. (2010, July 6). *Jersey Swaps, a Ritual With a Story*. The New York Times. https://www.nytimes.com/2010/07/07/sports/soccer/07jerseys.html

Wright, A. (2023, August 6). *"Even more proud to be Jamaican": Reggae Girlz defy the odds to reach World Cup knockout*. The Guardian. https://www.theguardian.com/football/2023/aug/06/even-more-proud-to-be-jamaican-reggae-girlz-defy-the-odds-to-reach-world-cup-knockout

Wyckoff, A. (2024, January 4). *Highest Scoring Soccer Games Ever*. Sportsnaut. https://sportsnaut.com/highest-scoring-soccer-games-ever/

Made in United States
Troutdale, OR
10/15/2024

23789221R00076